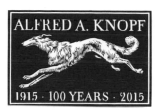

The First Book of Rhythms (1954)
The First Book of the Negroes (1952)
Pop and Fifina (1932) with Arna Bontemps

BIOGRAPHY AND AUTOBIOGRAPHY
Famous Negro Heroes of America (1958)
I Wonder as I Wander (1956)
Famous Negro Music Makers (1955)
Famous American Negroes (1954)
The Big Sea (1940)

ANTHOLOGY
*The Best Short Stories by Negro Writers: An Anthology
from 1899 to the Present* (1967)
New Negro Poets: USA (1964)
*An African Treasury: Articles / Essays / Stories / Poems
by Black Africans* (1960)
The Langston Hughes Reader (1958)
The Book of Negro Folklore (1958) with Arna Bontemps
Poetry of the Negro (1949) with Arna Bontemps

HISTORY
*Black Magic: A Pictorial History of the Negro in American
Entertainment* (1967) with Milton Meltzer
Fight for Freedom: The Story of the NAACP (1962)
A Pictorial History of the Negro in America (1956)
with Milton Meltzer

TRANSLATIONS
Selected Poems by Gabriela Mistral (1957)
Cuba Libre: Poems by Nicolás Guillén (1948)
Masters of the Dew (1947) with Mercer Cook. A translation of the novel
Gouverneurs de la rosée by Jacques Roumain

THE
WEARY
BLUES

THE
WEARY
BLUES

LANGSTON HUGHES

Introduction by CARL VAN VECHTEN

With a new Foreword by KEVIN YOUNG

NEW YORK : ALFRED A. KNOPF   2017

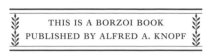

THIS IS A BORZOI BOOK
PUBLISHED BY ALFRED A. KNOPF

Copyright © 1926 by Alfred A. Knopf,
a division of Random House, LLC
Copyright renewed 1954 by Langston Hughes
Foreword copyright © 2015 by Kevin Young

www.aaknopf.com/poetry

Knopf, Borzoi Books, and the colophon are registered trademarks
of Random House LLC.

ISBN (hardcover) 978-0-385-35297-0
ISBN (eBook) 978-0-385-35298-7

Front-of-jacket image: Facsimile from the original 1926 design
by Miguel Covarrubias. Print courtesy of the Harry Ransom Center,
the University of Texas at Austin.

Manufactured in the United States of America

Published January 1926
Second Edition, February 10, 2015
Reprinted One Time
Third Printing, March 2017

TO MY MOTHER

I wish to thank the editors of *The Crisis,
Opportunity, Survey Graphic, Vanity Fair,
The World Tomorrow,* and *The Amsterdam
News* for having first published some of
the poems in this book.

CONTENTS

[xi]

FOREWORD

One never grows weary of *The Weary Blues*. Langston Hughes's first book, published by Knopf in 1926, is one of the high points of modernism and of what has come to be called the Harlem Renaissance—that flowering of African American literature and culture in the public's consciousness. Really an extension of the New Negro movement that began toward the start of the twentieth century, international as much as based in New York, the Harlem Renaissance represented different things to different people: to "race men" like W. E. B. DuBois and James Weldon Johnson, the black cultural ferment found from the teens to the nineteen twenties and beyond provided an opportunity to prove in culture things sometimes denied black folks in society—namely, their humanity.

For a younger generation of black artists like Hughes, their humanity proved self-evident. What's more, the freedom of expression they sought and Hughes insisted on in his 1926 manifesto "The Negro Artist and the Racial Mountain" didn't require putting a best foot forward in writing, or uplift in any easy sense. "We younger Negro artists who create now intend to express our individual dark-skinned selves without fear or shame," he wrote. "We know we are beautiful. And ugly too." As such, Hughes and other young writers often sought to scandalize as a form of sympathizing with those for whom life "ain't been no crystal stair." If Hughes's second book would take this as a kind of gospel, using the form of the blues to represent washwomen, porters, rounders, fools, and heroes—creating one of the best and most influential books of the twentieth century in the process—then _The Weary Blues_ represents the start of this newfound and profound blues and jazz aesthetic.

Hughes was in fact the first to write poetry in the blues form. He was the first to realize the blues are plural—to see in their complicated irony and earthy tone the potential to present a folk feeling both tragic and comic, one uniquely African American, which is to say, American. The blues made romance modern; modernism borrowed from the blues a new way of saying what it saw: Hughes made the blues his own, and ours too.

As I mention in my introduction to the Everyman's Pocket Poets volume _Blues Poems_ (2003), the form of the blues fights the feeling of the blues. If Hughes hasn't yet mined the blues form as fully in _The Weary Blues_ as he would later on, he has already embraced and in large part invented the blues aesthetic, "laughing to keep from crying":

> _Does a jazz-band ever sob?_
> _They say a jazz-band's gay._
> _Yet as the vulgar dancers whirled_
> _And the wan night wore away,_
> _One said she heard the jazz-band sob_
> _When the little dawn was grey._

The simplicity of this "Cabaret" may distract from the fact that jazz bands and vulgarity weren't easily found in poetry before Hughes wrote of them. Hughes's opening question here is well aware that what F. Scott Fitzgerald named the Jazz Age too often saw jazz bands as not only exclusively white but also relentlessly happy. By implying them black, and making their night not merely the fictional Great Gatsby's grand party but its wan aftermath, Hughes reveled in the gray (and gay) he saw around him in his travels to Mexico, his exile in Paris, and home in his adopted Harlem. "Show me a hero and I will write you a tragedy," Fitzgerald wrote. Hughes took tragedy and made it heroic, finding it comic too.

The Weary Blues also pioneers the jazz aesthetic. While others had earlier described jazz, often at a remove—notably Carl Sandburg in his "Jazz Fantasia"—Hughes knew that with jazz the form *is* the feeling. His poetry recognizes ecstasy not as a rarified state but a newborn freedom jazz helped him capture on the page. His first book is filled with exclamation points ("Sweet silver trumpets, / Jesus!") and typographical incursions ("Jazz-boys, jazz-boys,— / Play, plAY, PLAY!"); he even ends one poem simply: "!" He used this jazz aesthetic—one radical and racy and racial—to describe everything from a "Troubled Woman" to a "Danse Africaine." Sometimes this asymmetrical aesthetic is refined and refracted in short poems like "Winter Moon," quoted in full:

> *How thin and sharp is the moon tonight!*
> *How thin and sharp and ghostly white*
> *Is the slim curved crook of the moon tonight!*

Or take the enigmatic testimony of "Suicide's Note":

> *The calm,*
> *Cool face of the river*
> *Asked me for a kiss.*

From similar so-called American haiku Hughes would later craft his mid-career and mid-century masterpiece, *Montage of a Dream Deferred* (1951), which would give us quite a different Harlem in transition after the war, bringing bebop artistry to the page. In *The Weary Blues* he would first perfect that mix of hope with heartbreak—though individual poems may provide one or the other, as in his later book-length epic, they add up to a whole that truly sings.

Death is never far in this book, including in the title poem, which after a "Proem" (or prologue-poem) sets the scene, we find ourselves "Down on Lenox Avenue the other night" where the speaker watches a blues singer perform. The poem quotes the bluesman's song:

> *"I got the Weary Blues*
> *And I can't be satisfied.*
> *Got the Weary Blues*
> *And can't be satisfied—*
> *I ain't happy no mo'*
> *And I wish that I had died."*

The poem ends with a description of the singer who "slept like a rock or a man that's dead." Though in the end he's begun to identify with the singer, the "I" in the poem is still only an observer—but what an observer!—rather than the blues people that Hughes would regularly go on to speak as, and even for. This isn't to say that *The Weary Blues* isn't filled with personae (such as "When Sue Wears Red") or with nude dancers, beggar boys, cabaret singers, young sailors, and everyday folk who would dominate Hughes's further work. But it's the poems that speak of being "Black like me"—*black* still being fighting words in some quarters—that prove especially moving. Hughes manages remarkably to take Whitman's American "I" and write himself into it. After labeling the final section "Our Land," the volume ends with one of the more memorable lines of the century, almost an anthem: "I, too, am America."

Offering up a series of "Dream Variations," as one section is called, Hughes, it becomes clear, is celebrating, critiquing, and completing the American dream, that desire for equality or at least opportunity. But his America takes in the Americas—including Mexico, where his estranged father moved to flee the color line of the United States—and even the West Coast of Africa, which he'd also visited. His well-paced poetry is laced with an impeccable exile. *The Weary Blues* has so many now-classic verses that exemplify this it is hard to single out just one. But certainly we must mention "The Negro Speaks of Rivers," which, like the book's proem, manages to recast the "I" as racial and universal, declaring, "My soul has grown deep like the rivers." The first mature poem Hughes wrote (in 1920), here "Rivers" is dedicated to Du Bois; it is the poem he would end every reading with. Could it speak of the same river that had asked the suicide for a kiss? However mighty, this river, both real and metaphoric, flowed across and united a nation that, even if it didn't keep all its promises, still managed to hold out promise.

Writer Carl Van Vechten had helped guide Hughes's poems to Knopf, which would become his longtime publisher. But just as he would capitalize on seeing the popular poet Vachel Lindsay in a restaurant he worked in—playing up his being a newly "discovered" busboy poet, even though *The Weary Blues* was already in production—it was Hughes alone who made the most of such opportunities. Van Vechten and Hughes would remain close to the end of Hughes's life, but to call Van Vechten his patron is too reductive and elevating; to call him Hughes's mentor far too pat and patronizing. The two were that far more profound thing, friends. Van Vechten did provide an introduction to *The Weary Blues* (which follows in this anniversary edition), which, after it quotes heavily from Hughes's "picturesque" letters, perceptively notes his stanzas "have a highly deceptive air of spontaneous improvisation" that really is studied, almost presciently seeing their "expression of an essentially sensitive and subtly illusive nature, seeking always to break through the veil."

Hughes would provide Van Vechten a lens on and even access to a black world of "life behind the veil" that he sought the rest of his life to understand and that Hughes celebrated; and when Van Vechten's *Nigger Heaven* (1926) caused controversy from its title alone, Hughes would come to his defense under the same principle of artistic freedom that Hughes had asserted in "The Negro Artist." It would be the silhouetted cover of *The Weary Blues* by Mexico's Miguel Covarrubias that Hughes seemed more to mind. Suggested by Van Vechten, its iconic status now seems less an overwrought type, as it might have then, than a borrowing from the rather stately shadows of others—such as black artist Aaron Douglas, who like Hughes had lived as a child in Topeka, Kansas (where I once lived too) and with whom Hughes would collaborate over a long career.

Even given its rich context, *The Weary Blues* remains a unique achievement. A century after Knopf began as a publisher, and nearly ninety years after his book first appeared,

Hughes's innovation still resonates with its rich lines and fascinating lives—the very liveliness it brought to the world. His is a tremendous debut, and we are lucky to have it here in print again, exactly as Hughes wrote it, in all its black, blues, and symphonic glory.

—KEVIN YOUNG

Decatur, Georgia
September 6, 2014

INTRODUCING
LANGSTON HUGHES
TO THE READER

I

At the moment I cannot recall the name of any other person whatever who, at the age of twenty-three, has enjoyed so picturesque and rambling an existence as Langston Hughes. Indeed, a complete account of his disorderly and delightfully fantastic career would make a fascinating picaresque romance which I hope this young Negro will write before so much more befalls him that he may find it difficult to capture all the salient episodes within the limits of a single volume.

Born on February 1, 1902, in Joplin, Missouri, he had lived, before his twelfth year, in the City of Mexico, Topeka, Kansas, Colorado Springs, Charlestown, Indiana, Kansas City, and Buffalo. He attended Central High School, from which he graduated, at Cleveland, Ohio, while in the summer, there and in Chicago, he worked as delivery- and dummy-boy in hat-stores. In his senior year he was elected class poet and editor of the Year Book.

After four years in Cleveland, he once more joined his father in Mexico, only to migrate to New York where he entered Columbia University. There, finding the environment distasteful, or worse, he remained till spring, when he quit, broke with his father and, with thirteen dollars in cash, went on his own. First, he worked for a truck-farmer on Staten Island; next, he delivered flowers for Thorley; at length he partially satisfied an insatiable craving to go to sea by signing up with an old ship anchored in the Hudson for the winter. His first real cruise as a sailor carried him to the Canary Islands, the Azores, and the West Coast of Africa, of which voyage he has written: "Oh, the sun in Dakar! Oh, the little black girls of Burutu! Oh, the blue, blue bay of Loanda! Calabar, the city lost in a forest; the long, shining days at sea, the masts rocking against the stars at night; the black Kru-boy sailors, taken at Freetown, bathing on deck morning and evening; Tom Pey and Haneo, whose dangerous job it was to dive under the seven-ton mahogany logs floating and bobbing at the ship's side and fasten them to the chains of the crane; the vile houses of rotting women at Lagos; the desolation of the Congo; Johnny Walker, and the millions of whisky bottles buried in the sea along the West Coast; the daily fights on board, officers, sailors, everybody drunk; the timorous, frightened missionaries we carried as passengers; and George, the Kentucky colored boy, dancing and singing the Blues on the after-deck under the stars."

Returning to New York with plenty of money and a monkey, he presently shipped again—this time for Holland. Again he came back to New York and again he sailed—on his twenty-second birthday: February 1, 1924. Three weeks later he found himself in Paris with less than seven dollars. However, he was soon provided for: a woman of his own race engaged him as doorman at her *boîte de nuit*. Later he was employed, first as second cook, then as waiter, at the Grand Duc, where the Negro entertainer, Florence, sang at this epoch. Here he made friends with an Italian family who carried him off to their villa at Desenzano on Lago di Garda where he passed a happy month, followed by a night in Verona and a week in Venice. On his way back across Italy his passport was stolen and he became a beach-comber in Genoa. He has described his life there to me: "Wine and figs and *pasta*. And sunlight! And amusing companions, dozens of other beach-combers roving the dockyards and water-front streets, getting their heads whacked by the Fascisti, and breaking one loaf of bread into so many pieces that nobody got more than a crumb. I lived in the public gardens along the water-front and slept in the Albergo Populare for two lire a night amidst the snores of hundreds of other derelicts. . . . I painted my way home as a sailor. It seems that I must have painted the whole ship myself. We made a regular 'grand tour': Livorno, Napoli (we passed so close to Capri I could have cried). Then all around Sicily—Catania, Messina, Palermo— the Lipari Islands, miserable little peaks of pumice stone out in the sea; then across to Spain, divine Spain! My buddy and I went on a spree in Valencia for a night and a day. . . . Oh, the sweet wine of Valencia!"

He arrived in New York on November 10, 1924. That evening I attended a dance given in Harlem by the National Association for the Advancement of Colored People. Some time during the course of the night, Walter White asked me to meet two young Negro poets. He introduced me to Countée Cullen and Langston Hughes. Before that moment I had never heard of either of them.

·

II

I have merely sketched a primitive outline of a career as rich in adventures as a fruit-cake is full of raisins. I have already stated that I hope Langston Hughes may be persuaded to set it down on paper in the minutest detail, for the bull-fights in Mexico, the drunken gaiety of the Grand Duc, the delicately exquisite grace of the little black girls at Burutu, the exotic languor of the Spanish women at Valencia, the barbaric jazz dances of the cabarets in New York's own Harlem, the companionship of sailors of many races and nationalities, all have stamped an indelible impression on the highly sensitized, poetic imagination of this young Negro, an impression which has found its initial expression in the poems assembled in this book.

Motif of the nomad

And also herein may be discerned that nostalgia for color and warmth and beauty which explains this boy's nomadic instincts.

"We should have a land of sun,
Of gorgeous sun,
And a land of fragrant water
Where the twilight
Is a soft bandanna handkerchief
Of rose and gold,
And not this land where life is cold,"

he sings. Again, he tells his dream:

"To fling my arms wide
In the face of the sun,

Dance! whirl! whirl!
Till the quick day is done.
Rest at pale evening. . . .
A tall, slim tree. . . .
Night coming tenderly,
Black like me."

More of this wistful longing may be discovered in the poems entitled *The South* and *As I Grew Older.* His verses, however, are by no means limited to an exclusive mood; he writes caressingly of little black prostitutes in Harlem; his cabaret songs throb with the true jazz rhythm; his sea-pieces ache with a calm, melancholy lyricism; he cries bitterly from the heart of his race in *Cross* and *The Jester;* he sighs, in one of the most successful of his fragile poems, over the loss of a loved friend. Always, however, his stanzas are subjective, personal. They are the (I had almost said informal, for they have a highly deceptive air of spontaneous improvisation) expression of an essentially sensitive and subtly illusive nature, seeking always to break through the veil that obscures for him, at least in some degree, the ultimate needs of that nature.

To the Negro race in America, since the day when Phillis Wheatley indited lines to General George Washington and other aristocratic figures (for Phillis Wheatley never sang "My way's cloudy," or "By an' by, I'm goin' to lay down dis heavy load") there have been born many poets. Paul Laurence Dunbar, James Weldon Johnson, Claude McKay, Jean Toomer, Georgia Douglas Johnson, Countée Cullen, are a few of the more memorable names. Not the least of these names, I think, is that of Langston Hughes, and perhaps his adventures and personality offer the promise of as rich a fulfillment as has been the lot of any of the others.

—CARL VAN VECHTEN

New York
August 3, 1925

PROEM

"prologue poem"

Appositive style

I am a Negro:
    Black as the night is black,
    Black like the depths of my Africa.

I've been a slave:
    Cæsar told me to keep his door-steps clean.
    I brushed the boots of Washington.

invoking greatness — I was there.

Begin and End as a Negro

I've been a worker:
    Under my hand the pyramids arose.
    I made mortar for the Woolworth Building.

I've been a singer:
    All the way from Africa to Georgia
    I carried my sorrow songs.
    I made ragtime.

← slave songs

I've been a victim:
    The Belgians cut off my hands in the Congo.
    They lynch me now in Texas.

brutality

I am a Negro:
    Black as the night is black,
    Black like the depths of my Africa.

⌊1⌋

THE WEARY BLUES

THE WEARY BLUES

Droning a drowsy syncopated tune,   A
Rocking back and forth to a mellow croon,   A
    I heard a Negro play.   B
Down on Lenox Avenue the other night   C
By the pale dull pallor of an old gas light   C
    He did a lazy sway. . . .   B
    He did a lazy sway. . . .   B
To the tune o' those Weary Blues.
With his ebony hands on each ivory key
He made that poor piano moan with melody.
    O Blues!
Swaying to and fro on his rickety stool
He played that sad raggy tune like a musical fool.
    Sweet Blues!
Coming from a black man's soul.
    O Blues!
In a deep song voice with a melancholy tone
I heard that Negro sing, that old piano moan—
    "Ain't got nobody in all this world,
    Ain't got nobody but ma self.
    I's gwine to quit ma frownin'
    And put ma troubles on the shelf."
Thump, thump, thump, went his foot on the floor.
He played a few chords then he sang some more—
    "I got the Weary Blues
    And I can't be satisfied.
    Got the Weary Blues
    And can't be satisfied—
    I ain't happy no mo'
    And I wish that I had died."

observe (margin annotation)

[5]

high front vowel

And far into the night he crooned that tune.
The stars went out and so did the moon.
The singer stopped playing and went to bed
While the Weary Blues echoed through his head.
He slept like a rock or a man that's dead.

death

JAZZONIA

almost ode-like

Oh, silver tree!
Oh, shining rivers of the soul!

In a Harlem cabaret
Six long-headed jazzers play.
A dancing girl whose eyes are bold
Lifts high a dress of silken gold.

Prostitute as the Outsider

Oh, singing tree!
Oh, shining rivers of the soul!

Were Eve's eyes
In the first garden
Just a bit too bold?
Was Cleopatra gorgeous
In a gown of gold?

The Waste Land

Oh, shining tree!
Oh silver rivers of the soul!

In a whirling cabaret
Six long-headed jazzers play.

[7]

NEGRO DANCERS

"Me an' ma baby's
Got two mo' ways,
Two mo' ways to do de Charleston!
  Da, da,
  Da, da, da!
Two mo' ways to do de Charleston!"

Soft light on the tables,
Music gay,
Brown-skin steppers
In a cabaret.

White folks, laugh!
White folks, pray!

"Me an' ma baby's
Got two mo' ways,
Two mo' ways to do de Charleston!"

[8]

THE CAT AND THE SAXOPHONE
(2 A. M.)

EVERYBODY
Half-pint,—
Gin?
No, make it
LOVES MY BABY
corn.   You like
liquor,
don't you, honey?
BUT MY BABY
Sure.   Kiss me,
DON'T LOVE NOBODY
daddy.
BUT ME.
Say!
EVERYBODY
Yes?
WANTS MY BABY
I'm your
BUT MY BABY
sweetie, ain't I?
DON'T WANT NOBODY
Sure.
BUT
Then let's
ME,
do it!
SWEET ME.
Charleston,
mamma!
!

Read as a dialogue

YOUNG SINGER

One who sings "chansons vulgaires"
In a Harlem cellar
Where the jazz-band plays
From dark to dawn
Would not understand
Should you tell her
That she is like a nymph
For some wild faun.

CABARET

Does a jazz-band ever sob?
They say a jazz-band's gay.
Yet as the vulgar dancers whirled
And the wan night wore away,
One said she heard the jazz-band sob
When the little dawn was grey.

TO MIDNIGHT NAN AT LEROY'S

Strut and wiggle,
Shameless gal.
Wouldn't no good fellow
Be your pal.

Hear dat music. . . .
Jungle night.
Hear dat music. . . .
And the moon was white.

Sing your Blues song,
Pretty baby.
You want lovin'
And you don't mean maybe.

Jungle lover. . . .
Night black boy. . . .
Two against the moon
And the moon was joy.

Strut and wiggle,
Shameless Nan.
Wouldn't no good fellow
Be your man.

TO A LITTLE LOVER-LASS, DEAD

She
Who searched for lovers
In the night
Has gone the quiet way
Into the still,
Dark land of death
Beyond the rim of day.

Now like a little lonely waif
She walks
An endless street
And gives her kiss to nothingness.
Would God his lips were sweet!

HARLEM NIGHT CLUB

Sleek black boys in a cabaret.
Jazz-band, jazz-band,—
Play, plAY, PLAY!
Tomorrow. . . . who knows?
Dance today!

White girls' eyes
Call gay black boys.
Black boys' lips
Grin jungle joys.

Dark brown girls
In blond men's arms.
Jazz-band, jazz-band,—
Sing Eve's charms!

White ones, brown ones,
What do you know
About tomorrow
Where all paths go?

Jazz-boys, jazz-boys,—
Play, plAY, PLAY!
Tomorrow. . . . is darkness.
Joy today!

NUDE YOUNG DANCER

What jungle tree have you slept under,
Midnight dancer of the jazzy hour?
What great forest has hung its perfume
Like a sweet veil about your bower?

What jungle tree have you slept under,
Night-dark girl of the swaying hips?
What star-white moon has been your mother?
To what clean boy have you offered your lips?

YOUNG PROSTITUTE

Her dark brown face
Is like a withered flower
On a broken stem.
Those kind come cheap in Harlem
So they say.

TO A BLACK DANCER IN "THE LITTLE SAVOY"

Wine-maiden
Of the jazz-tuned night,
Lips
Sweet as purple dew,
Breasts
Like the pillows of all sweet dreams,
Who crushed
The grapes of joy
And dripped their juice
On you?

Isolation of sex

a question?

[17]

SONG FOR A BANJO DANCE

Shake your brown feet, honey,
Shake your brown feet, chile,
Shake your brown feet, honey,
Shake 'em swift and wil'—
    Get way back, honey,
    Do that low-down step.
    Walk on over, darling,
        Now! Come out
        With your left.
Shake your brown feet, honey,
Shake 'em, honey chile.

Sun's going down this evening—
Might never rise no mo'.
The sun's going down this very night—
Might never rise no mo'—
So dance with swift feet, honey,
    (The banjo's sobbing low)
Dance with swift feet, honey—
    Might never dance no mo'.

Shake your brown feet, Liza,
Shake 'em, Liza, chile,
Shake your brown feet, Liza,
    (The music's soft and wil')
Shake your brown feet, Liza,
    (The banjo's sobbing low)
The sun's going down this very night—
    Might never rise no mo'.

BLUES FANTASY

Hey!   Hey!
That's what the
Blues singers say.
Singing minor melodies
They laugh,
Hey!   Hey!

My man's done left me,
Chile, he's gone away.
My good man's left me,
Babe, he's gone away.
Now the cryin' blues
Haunts me night and day.

more of a call for help

Hey! ... Hey!

Weary,
Weary,
Trouble, pain.
Sun's gonna shine
Somewhere
Again.

I got a railroad ticket,
Pack my trunk and ride.

Sing 'em, sister!

Got a railroad ticket,
Pack my trunk and ride.

And when I get on the train
I'll cast my blues aside.
Laughing,
Hey! . . . Hey!
Laugh a loud,
Hey!   Hey!

LENOX AVENUE: MIDNIGHT

The rhythm of life
Is a jazz rhythm,
Honey.
The gods are laughing at us.

jazz is the rhythm of life," these poems are jazz influenced

The broken heart of love,
The weary, weary heart of pain,—
    Overtones,
    Undertones,
To the rumble of street cars,
To the swish of rain.

Lenox Avenue,
Honey.
Midnight,
And the gods are laughing at us.

DREAM VARIATIONS

DREAM VARIATION

To fling my arms wide
In some place of the sun,
To whirl and to dance
Till the white day is done.
Then rest at cool evening
Beneath a tall tree
While night comes on gently,
    Dark like me,—
That is my dream!

To fling my arms wide
In the face of the sun,
Dance! whirl! whirl!
Till the quick day is done.
Rest at pale evening. . . .
A tall, slim tree. . . .
Night coming tenderly
    Black like me.

[handwritten annotation:] The natural being home to the Black man

How thin and sharp is the moon tonight!
How thin and sharp and g<u>host</u>ly ⟨white⟩
Is the slim curved crook of the moon tonight!

poem of Fall

POÈME D'AUTOMNE

The autumn leaves
Are too heavy with color.
The slender trees
On the Vulcan Road
Are dressed in scarlet and gold
Like young courtesans
Waiting for their lovers.
But soon
The winter winds
Will strip their bodies bare
And then
The sharp, sleet-stung
Caresses of the cold
Will be their only
Love.

The weight of race in society

FANTASY IN PURPLE

Beat the drums of tragedy for me.
Beat the drums of tragedy and death.
And let the choir sing a stormy song
To drown the rattle of my dying breath.

Beat the drums of tragedy for me,
And let the (white) violins whir thin and slow,
But blow one blaring trumpet note of sun
To go with me
              to the darkness
                        where I go.

Decline, Continuity, transitoriness of life

MARCH MOON

The moon is naked.
The wind has undressed the moon.
The wind has blown all the cloud-garments
Off the body of the moon
And now she's naked,
Stark naked.

But why don't you blush,
O shameless moon?
Don't you know
It isn't nice to be naked?

Nakedness as Primitivism

JOY

I went to look for Joy,
Slim, dancing Joy,
Gay, laughing Joy,
Bright-eyed Joy,—
And I found her
Driving the butcher's cart
In the arms of the butcher boy!
Such company, such company,
As keeps this young nymph, Joy!

THE NEGRO SPEAKS OF RIVERS

THE NEGRO SPEAKS OF RIVERS

(To W. E. B. DuBois)

I've known rivers:
I've known rivers ancient as the world and older than the
flow of human blood in human veins.

My soul has grown deep like the rivers.

I bathed in the Euphrates when dawns were young.
I built my hut near the Congo and it lulled me to sleep.
I looked upon the Nile and raised the pyramids above it.
I heard the singing of the Mississippi when Abe Lincoln
went down to New Orleans, and I've seen its muddy
bosom turn all golden in the sunset.

I've known rivers:
Ancient, dusky rivers.

My soul has grown deep like the rivers.

CROSS

religious implication

My old man's a white old man
And my old mother's black.
If ever I cursed my white old man
I take my curses back.

If ever I cursed my black old mother
And wished she were in hell,
I'm sorry for that evil wish
And now I wish her well.

My old man died in a fine big house.
My ma died in a shack.
I wonder where I'm gonna die,
Being neither white nor black?

mixed racial identity

THE JESTER

In one hand
I hold tragedy
And in the other
Comedy,—
Masks for the soul.
Laugh with me.
You would laugh!
Weep with me.
You would weep!
Tears are my laughter.
Laughter is my pain.
Cry at my grinning mouth,
If you will.
Laugh at my sorrow's reign.
I am the Black Jester
The dumb clown of the world,
The booted, booted fool of silly men.
Once I was wise.
Shall I be wise again?

THE SOUTH

The lazy, laughing South
With blood on its mouth.
The sunny-faced South,
    Beast-strong,
    Idiot-brained.
The child-minded South
Scratching in the dead fire's ashes
For a Negro's bones.
    Cotton and the moon,
    Warmth, earth, warmth,
    The sky, the sun, the stars,
    The magnolia-scented South.
Beautiful, like a woman,
Seductive as a dark-eyed whore,
    Passionate, cruel,
    Honey-lipped, syphilitic—
    That is the South.
And I, who am black, would love her
But she spits in my face.
And I, who am black,
Would give her many rare gifts
But she turns her back upon me.
    So now I seek the North—
    The cold-faced North,
    For she, they say,
    Is a kinder mistress,
And in her house my children
May escape the spell of the South.

AS I GREW OLDER

It was a long time ago.
I have almost forgotten my dream.
But it was there then,
In front of me,
Bright like a sun,—
My dream.

And then the wall rose,
Rose slowly,
Slowly,
Between me and my dream.
Rose slowly, slowly,
Dimming,
Hiding,
The light of my dream.
Rose until it touched the sky,—
The wall.

Shadow.
I am black.

I lie down in the shadow.
No longer the light of my dream before me,
Above me.
Only the thick wall.
Only the shadow.

My hands!
My dark hands!
Break through the wall!

Find my dream!
Help me to shatter this darkness,
To smash this night,
To break this shadow
Into a thousand lights of sun,
Into a thousand whirling dreams
Of sun!

AUNT SUE'S STORIES

Aunt Sue has a head full of stories.
Aunt Sue has a whole heart full of stories.
Summer nights on the front porch
Aunt Sue cuddles a brown-faced child to her bosom
And tells him stories.

Black slaves
Working in the hot sun,
And black slaves
Walking in the dewy night,
And black slaves
Singing sorrow songs on the banks of a mighty river
Mingle themselves softly
In the flow of old Aunt Sue's voice,
Mingle themselves softly
In the dark shadows that cross and recross
Aunt Sue's stories.

And the dark-faced child, listening,
Knows that Aunt Sue's stories are real stories.
He knows that Aunt Sue
Never got her stories out of any book at all,
But that they came
Right out of her own life.

And the dark-faced child is quiet
Of a summer night
Listening to Aunt Sue's stories.

POEM

The night is beautiful,
So the faces of my people.

The stars are beautiful,
So the eyes of my people.

Beautiful, also, is the sun.
Beautiful, also, are the souls of my people.

Black is Beautiful.

BLACK PIERROT

A BLACK PIERROT

I am a black Pierrot:
    She did not love me,
    So I crept away into the night
    And the night was black, too.

I am a black Pierrot:
    She did not love me,
    So I wept until the red dawn
    Dripped blood over the eastern hills
    And my heart was bleeding, too.

I am a black Pierrot:
    She did not love me,
    So with my once gay-colored soul
    Shrunken like a balloon without air,
    I went forth in the morning
    To seek a new brown love.

HARLEM NIGHT SONG

Come,
Let us roam the night together
Singing.

I love you.

Across
The Harlem roof-tops
Moon is shining.
Night sky is blue.
Stars are great drops
Of golden dew.
In the cabaret
The jazz-band's playing.

I love you.

Come,
Let us roam the night together
Singing.

SONGS TO THE DARK VIRGIN

I

Would
That I were a jewel,
A shattered jewel,
That all my shining brilliants
Might fall at thy feet,
Thou dark one.

II

Would
That I were a garment,
A shimmering, silken garment,
That all my folds
Might wrap about thy body,
Absorb thy body,
Hold and hide thy body,
Thou dark one.

III

Would
That I were a flame,
But one sharp, leaping flame
To annihilate thy body,
Thou dark one.

ARDELLA

I would liken you
To a night without stars
Were it not for your eyes.
I would liken you
To a sleep without dreams
Were it not for your songs.

POEM

To the Black Beloved

Ah,
My black one,
Thou art not beautiful
Yet thou hast
A loveliness
Surpassing beauty.

Oh,
My black one,
Thou art not good
Yet thou hast
A purity
Surpassing goodness.

Ah,
My black one,
Thou art not luminous
Yet an altar of jewels,
An altar of shimmering jewels,
Would pale in the light
Of thy darkness,
Pale in the light
Of thy nightness.

WHEN SUE WEARS RED

When Susanna Jones wears red
Her face is like an ancient cameo
Turned brown by the ages.

Come with a blast of trumpets,
    Jesus!

When Susanna Jones wears red
A queen from some time-dead Egyptian night
Walks once again.

Blow trumpets, Jesus!

And the beauty of Susanna Jones in red
Burns in my heart a love-fire sharp like pain.

Sweet silver trumpets,
    Jesus!

PIERROT

I work all day,
Said Simple John,
Myself a house to buy.
I work all day,
Said Simple John,
But Pierrot wondered why.

For Pierrot loved the long white road,
And Pierrot loved the moon,
And Pierrot loved a star-filled sky,
And the breath of a rose in June.

I have one wife,
Said Simple John,
And, faith, I love her yet.
I have one wife,
Said Simple John,
But Pierrot left Pierrette.

For Pierrot saw a world of girls,
And Pierrot loved each one,
And Pierrot thought all maidens fair
As flowers in the sun.

Oh, I am good,
Said Simple John,
The Lord will take me in.
Yes, I am good,
Said Simple John,
But Pierrot's steeped in sin.

For Pierrot played on a slim guitar,
And Pierrot loved the moon,
And Pierrot ran down the long white road
With the burgher's wife one June.

WATER-FRONT STREETS

WATER-FRONT STREETS

The spring is not so beautiful there,—
    But dream ships sail away
To where the spring is wondrous rare
    And life is gay.

The spring is not so beautiful there,—
    But lads put out to sea
Who carry beauties in their hearts
    And dreams, like me.

A FAREWELL

With gypsies and sailors,
Wanderers of the hills and seas,
I go to seek my fortune.
With pious folk and fair
I must have a parting.
But you will not miss me,—
You who live between the hills
And have never seen the seas.

LONG TRIP

The sea is a wilderness of waves,
A desert of water.
We dip and dive,
Rise and roll,
Hide and are hidden
On the sea.
    Day, night,
    Night, day,
The sea is a desert of waves,
A wilderness of water.

PORT TOWN

Hello, sailor boy,
In from the sea!
Hello, sailor,
Come with me!

Come on drink cognac.
Rather have wine?
Come here, I love you.
Come and be mine.

Lights, sailor boy,
Warm, white lights.
Solid land, kid.
Wild, white nights.

Come on, sailor,
Out o' the sea.
Let's go, sweetie!
Come with me.

SEA CALM

How still,
How strangely still
The water is today.
It is not good
For water
To be so still that way.

CARIBBEAN SUNSET

God having a hemorrhage,
Blood coughed across the sky,
Staining the dark sea red,
That is sunset in the Caribbean.

YOUNG SAILOR

He carries
His own strength
And his own laughter,
His own today
And his own hereafter,—
This strong young sailor
Of the wide seas.

What is money for?
To spend, he says.
And wine?
To drink.
And women?
To love.
And today?
For joy.
And tomorrow?
For joy.
And the green sea
For strength,
And the brown land
For laughter.
And nothing hereafter.

SEASCAPE

Off the coast of Ireland
    As our ship passed by
We saw a line of fishing ships
    Etched against the sky.

Off the coast of England
    As we rode the foam
We saw an Indian merchantman
    Coming home.

NATCHA

Natcha, offering love.
For ten shillings offering love.
Offering: A night with me, honey.
A long, sweet night with me.
 Come, drink palm wine.
 Come, drink kisses.
A long, dream night with me.

SEA CHARM

Sea charm
The sea's own children
Do not understand.
They know
But that the sea is strong
Like God's hand.
They know
But that sea wind is sweet
Like God's breath,
And that the sea holds
A wide, deep death.

DEATH OF AN OLD SEAMAN

We buried him high on a windy hill,
But his soul went out to sea.
I know, for I heard, when all was still,
His sea-soul say to me:

Put no tombstone at my head,
For here I do not make my bed.
Strew no flowers on my grave,
I've gone back to the wind and wave.
Do not, do not weep for me,
For I am happy with my sea.

SHADOWS IN THE SUN

BEGGAR BOY

What is there within this beggar lad
That I can neither hear nor feel nor see,
That I can neither know nor understand
And still it calls to me?

Is not he but a shadow in the sun—
A bit of clay, brown, ugly, given life?
And yet he plays upon his flute a wild free tune
As if Fate had not bled him with her knife!

TROUBLED WOMAN

She stands
In the quiet darkness,
This troubled woman,
Bowed by
Weariness and pain,
Like an
Autumn flower
In the frozen rain.
Like a
Wind-blown autumn flower
That never lifts its head
Again.

SUICIDE'S NOTE

The calm,
Cool face of the river
Asked me for a kiss.

SICK ROOM

How quiet
It is in this sick room
Where on the bed
A silent woman lies between two lovers—
Life and Death,
And all three covered with a sheet of pain.

SOLEDAD

A Cuban Portrait

The shadows
Of too many nights of love
Have fallen beneath your eyes.
Your eyes,
So full of pain and passion,
So full of lies.
So full of pain and passion,
Soledad,
So deeply scarred,
So still with silent cries.

TO THE DARK MERCEDES OF "EL PALACIO DE AMOR"

Mercedes is a jungle-lily in a death house.
Mercedes is a doomed star.
Mercedes is a charnel rose.
Go where gold
Will fall at the feet of your beauty,
Mercedes.
Go where they will pay you well
For your loveliness.

MEXICAN MARKET WOMAN

This ancient hag
Who sits upon the ground
Selling her scanty wares
Day in, day round,
Has known high wind-swept mountains,
And the sun has made
Her skin so brown.

AFTER MANY SPRINGS

Now,
In June,
When the night is a vast softness
Filled with blue stars,
And broken shafts of moon-glimmer
Fall upon the earth,
Am I too old to see the fairies dance?
I cannot find them any more.

YOUNG BRIDE

They say she died,—
Although I do not know,
They say she died of grief
And in the earth-dark arms of Death
Sought calm relief,
And rest from pain of love
In loveless sleep.

THE DREAM KEEPER

Bring me all of your dreams,
You dreamers.
Bring me all of your
Heart melodies
That I may wrap them
In a blue cloud-cloth
Away from the too rough fingers
Of the world.

POEM

(To F. S.)

I loved my friend.
He went away from me.
There's nothing more to say.
The poem ends,
Soft as it began,—
I loved my friend.

OUR LAND

OUR LAND

Poem for a Decorative Panel

We should have a land of sun,
Of gorgeous sun,
And a land of fragrant water
Where the twilight
Is a soft bandanna handkerchief
Of rose and gold,
And not this land where life is cold.

We should have a land of trees,
Of tall thick trees
Bowed down with chattering parrots
Brilliant as the day,
And not this land where birds are grey.

Ah, we should have a land of joy,
Of love and joy and wine and song,
And not this land where joy is wrong.

Oh, sweet, away!
Ah, my beloved one, away!

LAMENT FOR DARK PEOPLES

I was a red man one time,
But the white men came.
I was a black man, too,
But the white men came.

They drove me out of the forest.
They took me away from the jungles.
I lost my trees.
I lost my silver moons.

Now they've caged me
In the circus of civilization.
Now I herd with the many—
Caged in the circus of civilization.

AFRAID

We cry among the skyscrapers
As our ancestors
Cried among the palms in Africa
Because we are alone,
It is night,
And we're afraid.

POEM

For the portrait of an African boy after the manner of
Gauguin

All the tom-toms of the jungles beat in my blood,
And all the wild hot moons of the jungles shine in my soul.
I am afraid of this civilization—
    So hard,
        So strong,
            So cold.

SUMMER NIGHT

The sounds
Of the Harlem night
Drop one by one into stillness.
The last player-piano is closed.
The last victrola ceases with the
"Jazz Boy Blues."
The last crying baby sleeps
And the night becomes
Still as a whispering heartbeat.
I toss
Without rest in the darkness,
Weary as the tired night,
My soul
Empty as the silence,
Empty with a vague,
Aching emptiness,
Desiring,
Needing someone,
Something.

I toss without rest
In the darkness
Until the new dawn,
Wan and pale,
Descends like a white mist
Into the court-yard.

DISILLUSION

I would be simple again,
Simple and clean
Like the earth,
Like the rain,
Nor ever know,
Dark Harlem,
The wild laughter
Of your mirth
Nor the salt tears
Of your pain.
Be kind to me,
Oh, great dark city.
Let me forget.
I will not come
To you again.

DANSE AFRICAINE

The low beating of the tom-toms,
The slow beating of the tom-toms,
    Low . . . slow
    Slow . . . low—
    Stirs your blood.
        Dance!
A night-veiled girl
    Whirls softly into a
    Circle of light.
    Whirls softly . . . slowly,
Like a wisp of smoke around the fire—
    And the tom-toms beat,
    And the tom-toms beat,
And the low beating of the tom-toms
    Stirs your blood.

THE WHITE ONES

I do not hate you,
For your faces are beautiful, too.
I do not hate you,
Your faces are whirling lights of loveliness and splendor,
     too.
Yet why do you torture me,
O, white strong ones,
Why do you torture me?

MOTHER TO SON

Well, son, I'll tell you:
Life for me ain't been no crystal stair.
It's had tacks in it,
And splinters,
And boards torn up,
And places with no carpet on the floor—
Bare.
But all the time
I'se been a-climbin' on,
And reachin' landin's,
And turnin' corners,
And sometimes goin' in the dark
Where there ain't been no light.
So boy, don't you turn back.
Don't you set down on the steps
'Cause you finds it's kinder hard.
Don't you fall now—
For I'se still goin', honey,
I'se still climbin',
And life for me ain't been no crystal stair.

POEM

We have tomorrow
Bright before us
Like a flame.

Yesterday
A night-gone thing,
A sun-down name.

And dawn-today
Broad arch above the road we came.

EPILOGUE

I, too, sing America.

I am the darker brother.
They send me to eat in the kitchen
When company comes,
But I laugh,
And eat well,
And grow strong.

Tomorrow,
I'll sit at the table
When company comes.
Nobody'll dare
Say to me,
"Eat in the kitchen,"
Then.

Besides,
They'll see how beautiful I am
And be ashamed,—

I, too, am America.

Langston Hughes was born in Joplin, Missouri, in 1902. After graduation from high school, he spent a year in Mexico with his father, then a year studying at Columbia University. His first poem in a nationally known magazine was "The Negro Speaks of Rivers," which appeared in *Crisis* in 1921. In 1925, he was awarded the First Prize for Poetry from the magazine *Opportunity* for "The Weary Blues," which gave its title to his first book of poems, published in 1926. Hughes received his B.A. from Lincoln University in Pennsylvania in 1929. In 1943, he was awarded an honorary Litt.D. by his alma mater; during his lifetime, he was also awarded a Guggenheim Fellowship (1935), a Rosenwald Fellowship (1940), and an American Academy of Arts and Letters Grant (1947). From 1926 until his death in 1967, Hughes devoted his time to writing and lecturing. He wrote poetry, short stories, autobiography, song lyrics, essays, humor, and plays. A cross-section of his work was published in 1958 as *The Langston Hughes Reader;* a *Selected Poems* first appeared in 1959, and a *Collected Poems* in 1994 Today, his many works and his contribution to American letters continue to be cherished and celebrated around the world.

A NOTE ON THE TYPE

This book was set in a modern adaptation of a type designed by the first William Caslon (1692–1766). The Caslon face, an artistic, easily read type, has enjoyed over two centuries of popularity in our own country. It is of interest to note that the first copies of the Declaration of Independence and the first paper currency distributed to the citizens of the newborn nation were printed in this typeface.

Typeset by Scribe, Philadelphia, Pennsylvania

Printed and bound by Thomson Shore, Dexter, Michigan

Designed by Maggie Hinders